Celebrating the Family Name of Peters

Walter the Educator

Silent King Books
a WhichHead Entertainment Imprint

Celebrating the Family Name of Peters is a memory book that belongs to the Celebrating Family Name Book Series by Walter the Educator. Collect them all and more books at WaltertheEducator.com

USE THE EXTRA SPACE TO DOCUMENT YOUR FAMILY MEMORIES THROUGHOUT THE YEARS

PETERS

The name of Peters, bold and true,

Through years and miles, it still renews.

With roots that run both deep and far,

They shine as bright as any star.

With hands that build and hearts that care,

The Peters family stands aware.

In every land they've made their mark,

Their spirits brave, their vision stark.

Through trials met with steady grace,

They find their strength in each embrace.

With laughter rich and courage wide,

They face the world, side by side.

Each generation, bold and wise,

A legacy that never dies.

From past to present, future bright,

The Peters name is purest light.

Through quiet fields or bustling town,

Their pride and purpose pass down.

In every task, in work or play,

The Peters strength lights up the way.

With gentle hands and thoughtful mind,

They're seekers, builders, true and kind.

In all they do, in all they give,

They show the world just how to live.

For honor's weight they hold with care,

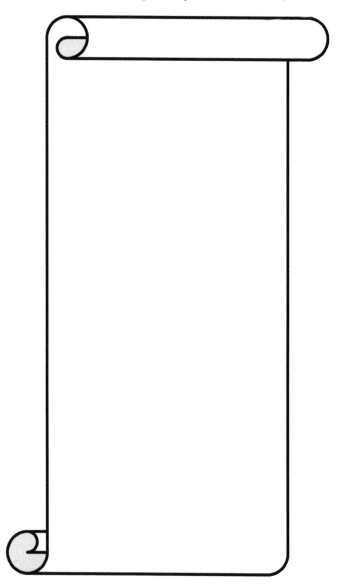

And rise together, everywhere.

A family woven strong and tight,

In unity, they find their might.

Their story told through deeds, not fame,

The Peters live up to their name.

In simple joys, in labors long,

They build a world both safe and strong.

Through winds of change and shifting sands,

They hold together, hand in hand.

The Peters bond, a steadfast chain,

Through sun and storm, through joy and pain.

So let the name of Peters ring,

A song of courage, strength, and spring.

For they endure, they rise, they stand

A proud, resilient, lasting band.

ABOUT THE CREATOR

Walter the Educator is one of the pseudonyms for Walter Anderson. Formally educated in Chemistry, Business, and Education, he is an educator, an author, a diverse entrepreneur, and he is the son of a disabled war veteran. "Walter the Educator" shares his time between educating and creating. He holds interests and owns several creative projects that entertain, enlighten, enhance, and educate, hoping to inspire and motivate you. Follow, find new works, and stay up to date with Walter the Educator™

at WaltertheEducator.com